Learning and Living God's Word

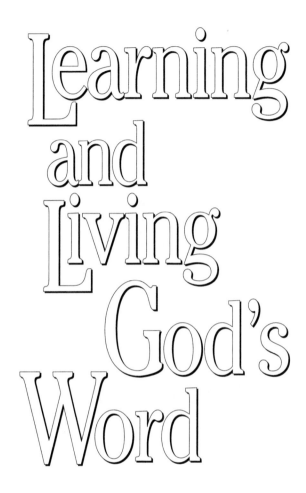

Learning and Living God's Word

DANIEL J. ESTES

REGULAR BAPTIST PRESS
1300 North Meacham Road
Schaumburg, Illinois 60173-4806

Library of Congress Cataloging-in-Publication Data

Estes, Daniel J., 1953–
    Learning and living God's word / Daniel J. Estes.
      p. cm.
    ISBN 0–87227–181–1
    1. Bible—Study and teaching.   I. Title.
BS600.2.E85   1993
220' .07—dc20   93-42420
                                                         CIP

LEARNING AND LIVING GOD'S WORD

© 1993
Regular Baptist Press • Schaumburg, Illinois
1-800-727-4440 • www.regularbaptistpress.org
Printed in U.S.A.
RBP5218 • ISBN: 0-87227-181-1
Third printing—2003

Contents

How to Use This Book 7

1   Getting a Good Start 9

2   Formulating a Framework 17

3   Looking Through the Microscope 25

4   Digging into Words 31

5   Seeing the Structure 39

6   Summarizing the Subject 47

7   Expressing the Idea 53

8   Building a Bridge 59

9   Living What We Learn 67

10   Staying in the Word 73

Glossary 77

How to Use This Book

Learning and Living God's Word is a special kind of book. It is not a novel with a gripping story to read. Neither is it a textbook with facts to memorize. It is a manual—a workbook designed to teach you how to study the Bible on your own. This book will guide you into the skills you need to learn and live God's Word. It was born out of a small group study in my church, after five young couples asked me to teach them the skills of personal Bible study. Whether you are a teen, a college student or an older adult, this manual can help you.

I have prepared this manual with many different people in mind. It is the kind of book I needed when I first tried to study the Bible on my own as a high school student. This manual presents the skills that I have taught to ten years of students at Cedarville College. They, in turn, have taken the material back to their churches and around the world on missions trips.

With all of the books on Bible study available today, what makes *Learning and Living God's Word* different?

First, it is personal. You can use this book to teach yourself. Be sure to complete the practice exercises and then to reflect on the questions at the end of each chapter. You will be surprised at how quickly your skills will grow!

Second, it is practical. Many Bible study books are excellent in theory, but they do not teach you how to make the theory work out in practice. This manual focuses on developing your skills. It does not stop with exhorting you about *what* you ought to do. It explains *how* to do it.

Third, it is flexible. It works as a self-study program. However, a teacher can use it in a class of teens, college students or adults. In addition, home Bible study groups can work their way through the manual. It is a user-friendly method that really works.

I trust that God will use this book to teach you the dynamic, life-changing skill of Bible study. May He bless you in *Learning and Living God's Word.*

Lesson 1

Getting a Good Start

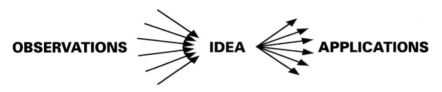

OBSERVATIONS ➤ **IDEA** ◀ **APPLICATIONS**

Why Should We Study the Bible?

With so many books to choose from, why study the Bible? After all, it is a long and ancient book that refers to times and nations unfamiliar to the modern reader. Why *should* we study the Bible?

For many people the Bible is worthy of study because of the profound influence it has had on world literature and culture. The stirring dramas of Shakespeare and the lofty poetry of Milton repeatedly allude to Biblical events and characters. Many authors, even in contemporary times, develop themes that find their source in the Bible. To understand much of European and American art, music and literature, people need a basic knowledge of the Bible.

Others recognize the influence the Bible has had on the laws, values and thinking of our society. Politicians and educators frequently point to the Bible to support their positions. The Bible has been brought into recent social discussions, such as abortion, women's rights, capital punishment and apartheid.

These uses of the Bible alone would justify its study. However, the Christian has even more important reasons. We find **three** of these **reasons** in 2 Timothy 3:16 and 17. First, we should study the Bible because it is God's Word to us. Paul stated in 2 Timothy 3:16 that all Scripture is inspired by God. The word "inspired" means literally "God-breathed." The Bible is God speaking to us. It is what God wants us to know. When we study the Bible, we are listening to God's voice. If the Bible was important enough for God to say, it is certainly important enough for us to listen. We should study the Bible because as God's Word it is **important.**

Second, the Bible has **several benefits** for those who study it. Because the Scripture is inspired by God, it is profitable for *teaching*, that is, for positive instruction concerning God and His will. In the Bible, God tells us who He is, who we are and what He wants us to do. The Bible is also beneficial for *reproof*, or for negative admonition pointing out our sins and inadequacies. Like a doctor, it diagnoses our spiritual diseases and points us to our needs. In addition, it *corrects* us by giving direction about getting back to God's way. The Bible is like a coach who tells the team how they can correct the mistakes that have caused them to lose a game. Furthermore, the Bible *trains* in righteousness by giving continuing direction for living in accordance with God's standard. It cheers us on as we seek to live in a way that pleases God. We should study the Bible because of its benefits.

Third, all of these benefits have a larger **goal,** which is spelled out in 2 Timothy 3:17: "That the man of God may be adequate, equipped for every good work" (NASB). The word "adequate" refers to fitness. The ultimate purpose of Bible study is not just knowing a lot of facts; it is our spiritual fitness. When we hear and obey God's Word, we get into spiritual shape so that we can do what God wants us to do. God's Word equips us to do God's work.

Although the Bible is an important piece of literature that has influenced the Western world, its significance is even greater for the Christian. As Christians, we study the Bible because God has spoken to us through it. As we study the Bible, God teaches us, reproves us, corrects us and trains us. In the end we become spiritually fit to do His work. These are the primary reasons why Christians should study the Bible.

How Should We Study the Bible?

As a young Christian I was encouraged to study the Bible, but no one gave me much instruction on how to do it. I can remember picking up a few hints from Sunday School papers, sermons and youth club talks, but no one ever showed me how to take a passage of the Bible, study it carefully, understand it clearly and apply it appropriately. My well-intentioned teachers were long on exhortation, but short on explanation.

For years I floundered through repeated attempts to study the Bible, each time giving up in frustration. After talking with many people over the past ten years, I have concluded that this frustration was not unique to me. Many Christians want to study the Bible for themselves, but they just do not know how. They have sufficient desire, but they need some clear direction. In fact, this problem is not limited to young Christians. Many godly believers who have served the Lord for years will confess that when it comes to studying the Bible, they are lost or at least wandering around in circles.

Although people attempt to study the Bible by numerous means, Bible study falls into three general categories. Each of these procedures has benefits but also some limitations.

The first common procedure is the **analytical** approach, or what we may call the "telephone directory" type of Bible study. Telephone directories have a lot of facts but no overall plot. The student who follows this approach analyzes in minute detail the words of the text and compiles lists of observations about what he finds. Some pastors and teachers use this method in their ministries. When you come out of one of their sermons or classes, you may feel as if you've tried to sip water out of a fire hose! You may have heard about things such as aorists, hiphils and the Jebusites, but you ended up with no clear idea of the passage's meaning or application.

Certainly the analytical method has the benefit of seeking the precise understanding of the words used in the Bible, and it trains the reader in the skill of careful observation of what God said. However, by focusing exclusively on the details, the student may well miss the bigger picture. This lack may move him in the direction of imbalanced doctrine, because he does not consider how other passages in the Bible may balance the verse he is studying. Many false beliefs start in this way. A reader blows out of proportion a word, verse or concept and ignores the rest of Scripture. In addition, he may have a difficult time relating his observations to contemporary life. The analytical procedure is great for seeing the details, but it often seems piecemeal and irrelevant to life today.

A second type of procedure is the **devotional** approach, or what we may call the "wishing well" technique. With this procedure, the reader goes to the text in order to find some blessing or instruction for his own life, but he is unconcerned with what the text means in and of itself. He wants the Bible only to encourage or direct him for the day. Not surprisingly, this search often brings personal blessing to the reader, for the Bible seems to relate in specific ways to his personal needs.

Nevertheless, such devotional use of the Bible has some limitations. Devotional reading may misuse the text by twisting it to address directly the reader's questions. Instead of listening to what the Bible says to him, the devotional reader may reinterpret the Bible to say what he wants to hear. Consequently, though the reader may indeed find many truths that *seem* to apply to his life, the nagging question persists, "Is that what God really said, or is that what I made up myself?" Thus he may lack confidence that his application is truly what the text means. Even though the devotional method seems highly applicable, it may actually produce hesitancy to put one's whole weight on the "applications" he has found.

The third common procedure in Bible study consists of "peeking over the shoulder" of **commentaries**, tapes, videos or sermons. Instead of studying the Bible for himself, the individual depends upon what others have written or said. No doubt, this method often results in accurate interpretation; and in many cases the sources suggest meaningful, specific applications. After all, good sermons and books are written by people who have spent years in developing their skills in understanding the Bible. They may know the original languages in which the Bible was written and be familiar with a range of interpretations and arguments about the passage. In addition, skillful Bible teachers and writers are effective because they are keen observers of life. Therefore, their messages are filled with helpful, relevant applications for life today.

However, relying on someone else's study is much like kissing through a pane of glass—you get the same general idea, but you miss the personal excitement! When someone else studies the Bible and then tells us what he found, we do not get to enjoy discovering God's truth for ourselves. In addition, getting God's Word through a third party may well cause us to be less likely to obey God's truth. The Bible is most compelling when we hear the message for ourselves. The commentary approach may be highly accurate and applicable, but it leaves us a step away from hearing God's Word ourselves.

What Do We Need?

We need a technique for Bible study that builds on the benefits of the procedures but avoids their limitations. In addition, it must be efficient enough to fit into people's fast-paced lives, and flexible enough for use with the various types of literature in the Bible.

The ideal procedure of Bible study has four major components. First, it must yield **maximum accuracy**. If the Bible is God's Word, we must not remain content to get just the gist of its message. Our Bible study must be accurate enough to handle the details of God's message. Second, we want to attain **maximum application**. It is not good enough to know what the Bible said to people thousands of years ago in a culture far different from ours. Bible study has to be relevant; it needs to address life today. Third, our method needs to retain for us the **joy of personal discovery**. Fourth, our process will be most useful if we can use it within a **reasonable time**. The technique developed in this manual meets all four of these objectives.

How Does It Work?

The Bible study procedure in this book is called the inductive process of Bible study. We can visualize it with the following chart:

The technique begins with **observations** of the Biblical text. These observations help us to understand in precise terms what the passage meant when it was originally written within the context of the ancient world. This first step involves the observation of both the words used and the structure that links the words together.

This initial step of observation by itself produces only analysis. By looking at the passage in detail, we discern many pieces of data. This data is disconnected; therefore, it does not give us a clear understanding of the writer's message. In scrutinizing each individual tree, we may well lose the larger picture of the forest.

The second major step tries to synthesize the passage. This step draws together the random observations we have accumulated in the process of observation. As a result, we articulate the **central idea** of the passage. The idea endeavors to represent accurately and succinctly the writer's emphasis to his original audience.

The final step focuses upon **applications**. We use the central idea of the passage to illuminate many areas of life today with specific, measurable applications. Applications may address many different target audiences, but we must measure their appropriateness by analyzing the relationship between the original audience and the specific target audience.

Each of these three steps of Bible study is built upon an implication drawn from the Bible. Observation recognizes that the Bible was originally written in the language of common people because God wanted to make His truth available to all. The premise of the idea step is that the Bible is a piece of literature organized into coherent units containing one key idea each. The process of application holds that the Bible as God's timeless truth speaks to lives today in conjunction with its message to the original audience.

As we study the Bible, we have the great resource of the teaching ministry of the Holy Spirit. As Jesus stated in John 16:13, He gave the Spirit of God to guide us into all truth. In our study of God's Word, we must give our best effort, but at the same time we must depend upon the Holy Spirit's teaching.

Key Points to Remember

- According to 2 Timothy 3:16 and 17, we should study the Bible because
  - it is **important:** God said it, so we should listen to it;
  - it is **beneficial:** it teaches, reproves, corrects, and trains us;
  - it develops **our spiritual fitness:** God's Word equips us to do God's work.
- Common procedures of Bible study have **benefits** and **limitations:**
  - **analytical procedure** sees the details, but misses the whole picture and the application;
  - **devotional procedure** applies to life, but it may misuse the text;
  - **commentary procedure** may be accurate and applicable, but it does not give the joy of personal discovery.
- The **ideal procedure** of Bible study (inductive Bible study) seeks
  - maximum **accuracy;**

- maximum **application;**
- **joy** of personal discovery;
- reasonable **time** commitment.

Questions for Reflection

1. Which of the benefits of Bible study listed in 2 Timothy 3:16 do you need most in your life now? Why?

2. How would you describe your spiritual fitness at this time? What areas of your life do you need to shape up?

3. How confident are you in your present approach to Bible study?

4. Which of the common procedures of Bible study have you used most?

5. How can the inductive process of Bible study help you?

Lesson 2

Formulating a Framework

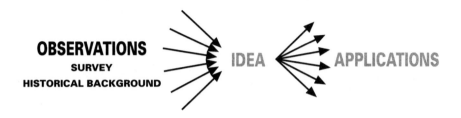

OBSERVATIONS
SURVEY
HISTORICAL BACKGROUND
IDEA
APPLICATIONS

Looking at the Big Picture

How do you read a book? For most people, reading a book means starting at page 1 and wading through the entire volume until the end. This plan sounds sensible enough, but is it necessarily the best way to read a book?

The problem in reading an unfamiliar work, such as one of the books in the Bible, is that we sometimes see only the trees and miss the forest in the process. Consequently, we may not recognize the full significance of the individual parts because we see the details in isolation instead of in their relationship within the total work. When we lose the big picture, we can easily become frustrated and give up in our study.

Therefore, it helps to begin reading a book by seeing it as a whole before we try to examine it in minute detail. To do this, we must survey the book. **Survey reading** of a book of the Bible should take no more than five minutes. In that short time, we want to form an initial impression of the book. By skimming through the book and noting significant features such as the introductory verses, the beginning and the end of chapters and the concluding verses, we can develop a general feel for the book. Survey reading is like being a detective who first looks for the obvious clues to help solve the case.

By the end of this short survey, we will understand in general terms what the book refers to, what type of literature it is and why it was written. Of course, additional intensive study may alter these initial impressions. Nevertheless, survey reading helps us to get a general feel for the book, before the details overwhelm and discourage us.

EXAMPLE

Survey Reading of Philippians

- This is a brief, warm letter from Paul to the Philippian church.
- Paul was in prison, but he maintained a joyful attitude.
- Several times Paul talked about the need for unity.
- Paul mentioned a number of people by name.
- Paul wanted to encourage the Philippians to have a Christlike attitude toward one another.

Now You Try It!

1. Choose a book of the Bible that is unfamiliar to you.
2. Take five minutes to survey the book. Skim the first few verses of each chapter and read the book's introduction and conclusion.
3. Record your initial impressions:

What does the book refer to?

What kind of literature is it?

Why was this book written?

When Was the Book Written, and Why?

Before we can understand the Bible as it addresses the here and now, we must understand what it meant there and then, when it was originally written. Unfortunately, most of the books of the Bible do not state clearly who wrote them and why. Occasionally, a verse such as John 20:31 will spell out the Biblical writer's purpose in composing the book, but for the most part the purpose is only implied. However, a sensitive, careful reading of a book will often yield information about its historical background.

After the initial survey reading, or pre-reading, we need to examine the whole book more carefully. We may focus on just a short passage of Scripture in our study, but we need to grasp the meaning of the context of that passage. This stage of our study is reading for the **historical background,** or superficial reading.

In **superficial reading,** we need to read straight through the book in one sitting, without stopping to ponder what we do not understand right away. The purpose of this reading is to understand the big picture. Therefore, we have to be careful not to get bogged down in the details. We will have ample opportunity to examine them later!

When we work on a jigsaw puzzle, we usually try to put together the border first. We could possibly complete the puzzle by starting with the center pieces; but the border helps, for it provides an outline, or a framework for fitting the other pieces together. When we read for the historical background, we are constructing an initial framework of understanding for interpreting the book's details.

This framework is really an informed hypothesis—an educated guess—of the original situation that the writer addressed. Most of the Bible was originally intended for specific occasions. For example, Paul wrote 1 Corinthians in response to a list of questions that the church at Corinth had sent him (1 Cor 7:1). We read the Biblical book as though we are listening to one end of a telephone conversation. From that one-sided conversation, we try to infer the writer's intention in the original situation.

Sometimes, other books of the Bible can help us to understand the historical background. The historical books of Kings and Chronicles are the backdrop for the Old Testament prophetic books. Obscure references in books such as Isaiah and Jeremiah suddenly come to light when we compare passages in the historical books. In the New Testament, the book of Acts provides many interpretive keys for Paul's epistles. The more we know about the Bible in general, the more help we have to draw on in understanding the original context of the individual books in the Bible.

Making wise use of work done by specialists can help us. Reference Bibles often include a short introduction to each book of the Bible. In addition, Bible dictionaries, handbooks and commentaries contain useful discussions of how the book came to be written. We should not use these helps as crutches. That would be the commentary approach, which relies too much on the work of others. However, it is profitable to use them as aids to assist our understanding.

In our superficial reading, we will note some explicit statements about the historical background. These statements are there in the text in black and white. In addition, as we read sensitively between the lines, we will detect implied clues. Sometimes we can learn something about the *writer,* his identity and his relationship to the readers. Many books specify their *recipients.* Listening to the writer's side of the conversation many times helps us to reconstruct what the recipients must have thought and said. Frequently, the books give clues as to the *situation* that prompted the writing. In addition, we can usually learn much about the author's *purpose, theme* and *tone.* At this point, it is helpful to record what we have found about the historical background in our superficial reading.

EXAMPLE
Historical Background of Colossians
Writer
- The apostle Paul wrote the book of Colossians.
- Paul wrote from prison about A.D. 60.
- Paul was struggling for the Colossians and for the Laodiceans.
- Paul, as far as we know, had never visited the church at Colosse (2:1).

Recipients
- Paul wrote to the holy and faithful believers in Christ at Colosse (1:2).
- Paul greeted Nympha and the brothers in Laodicea (4:15, 16).
- Paul also sent a message for Archippus (4:17).

Situation
- Paul wrote this letter at a time when false teachers were in Colosse (2:4, 8, 20–23).
- The Colossian church was large and influential. It probably was made up of many Gentile converts and also some Jews.

Purpose
- Paul wanted to show that Christ is preeminent, supreme over everything (1:15–17).
- Paul wanted the Colossians to know that the Christian's life should reflect this priority (1:22).
- Paul wanted to let them know that Christ's death was all they needed—they were free from man-made rules (2:20–23).
- Paul wrote to exhort them to a life of holiness (3:1–17).

Theme
- Colossians portrays the Church of Christ.
- Colossians focuses on Christ, the Head of the Church (1:18).

Tone
- Paul wrote in a warm tone of greeting, letting the believers know that he prayed for them at all times (1:3; 2:5).
- Paul wrote in a tone of warning against false teachers (2:8).

Now You Try It!
1. Use the book of Philippians for your historical background search.
2. Read through the book in one sitting, trying to understand the original situation in which the apostle wrote the book.
3. Record the explicit statements and implied clues you find. Whenever possible, document your observations by citing the references in the Bible.

Writer (his identity, his characteristics, his location, his relationship to the readers, etc.)

Recipients (their identity, their location, their spiritual condition, their questions and needs, etc.)

Situation (events occurring at that time, time of prosperity or persecution, etc.)

Purpose (why the writer wrote the book)

Theme (the general subject matter)

Tone (what tone of voice the writer likely used)

Survey reading and superficial reading are only the initial steps of observation. They serve to give us a general impression of the book as a whole. Now we are ready to turn on the microscope and look in detail at the text.

Key Points to Remember

Survey reading is like being a detective. We first look for the obvious clues in order to form an initial impression of the book in no more than five minutes.

Superficial reading (learning the **historical background**) helps us to develop an interpretive framework for understanding the book.

- Read straight through the book to get the big picture, not for details.
- Make an informed hypothesis of the original situation.
- If you can, use information from other Biblical books.
- Use the work of specialists as an aid, but not as a crutch.
- Write down explicit statements and implied clues that you find in the following categories: author, purpose, recipients, theme, situation and tone.

Questions for Reflection

1. Why is it important to grasp the big picture before you get into the details of a passage of Scripture?

2. Have you used survey and superficial reading in the past? Why or why not?

3. Does studying an unfamiliar book of the Bible intimidate you? Why or why not?

4. How can a good general knowledge of the Bible help you in your more detailed study of a passage of Scripture?

5. How can you wisely use others' works in your Bible study?

Looking Through the Microscope

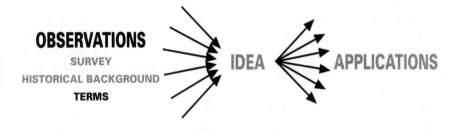

OBSERVATIONS
SURVEY
HISTORICAL BACKGROUND
TERMS

IDEA

APPLICATIONS

What Does That Word Mean?

How do we determine what a word means? Does a word always have the same meaning? Suppose, for example, I instructed you, "Put the trunk into the trunk." You might assume that I meant you should place a suitcase into the back of a car. Certainly, that could be my intention, but did I necessarily want to communicate that idea? The dictionary lists seventeen uses of the word "trunk" in the English language. Consequently, there are 17 times 17, or 289, possible meanings for the instruction, "Put the trunk into the trunk."

In a similar way, Biblical terms have the potential for many different meanings. How can we determine what a word means in a particular verse of the Bible?

The understanding of terms begins with the observation of the **morphemes** that form words. A morpheme is a basic building block of meaning, just as a phoneme is the basic building block of sound. Briefly defined, a morpheme is a word or part of a word that has specific meaning. For example, the word "dogs" has two morphemes: *dog* represents a specific type of four-footed mammal, and *s* represents a plural number. The combination of the meanings of both morphemes determines the total meaning of the word "dogs." The word "jumped" also has two morphemes: *jump,* which defines a type of action, and the past tense indicator *-ed.* Both morphemes contribute to the total meaning of the word. Most words have only one morpheme, but we must be alert to some words that contain several meaningful parts.

We have seen from the example of "trunk" that words can often represent several meanings. The total quantity that a morpheme could possibly represent in a language is called the **semantic range**. For example, the term "trust" in English has a semantic range that includes eleven different uses.

Several factors make the precise understanding of a specific Biblical term in a verse difficult. Words and concepts rarely coincide. A word is capable of multiple meanings, with each meaning having a different set of synonyms. It is not enough to say that a particular word equals a specific concept. Words are much more complex than that.

In addition, the Bible was originally written in three languages different from English: Hebrew, Aramaic and Greek. The terms in these languages also have ranges of meaning. Therefore, to understand what the term could mean in the Biblical context we are studying, we must determine the semantic range of the morpheme within the *writer's* original language. Thus, the task of Bible study is exegesis, leading out the writer's meaning, not eisegesis, reading in the reader's conceptions.

Obviously the specific meaning of a term used in a particular passage does not mean everything that the word could possibly mean. When I say, "Put the trunk into the trunk," I do not mean all 289 possible renderings of the expression. Therefore, specific meaning does not coincide with semantic range.

Different writers may **use** the same term differently. For example, in America "boot" refers to an overshoe, but in Britain the boot is the luggage compartment of a car. In a similar way, Paul in Ephesians 2:9 used the term "works" with a different nuance from that which James used in James 2:14. For the most part, Biblical words, like words in any language, are not well-defined technical terms, even in the original Biblical languages. We must carefully examine the context of the term to determine the specific meaning intended by the writer in the individual case.

The following chart illustrates the relationship between the semantic range, the usage and the writer's specific meaning:

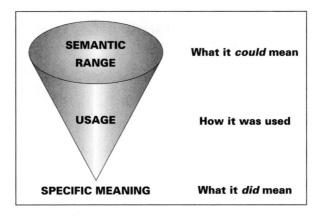

To discover the intended meaning, the near context is the most helpful indicator. By taking into account the argument of the surrounding passage, the writer's tone and the original audience, we can narrow the potential meaning of the specific term. In this way, we can determine the likely meaning of the term in the specific passage with a high degree of probability.

EXAMPLE
Observations of Proverbs 3:5 and 6

- The son was to trust in the Lord.
- He was to trust in the Lord with *all* of his heart.
- The son was not to lean on his own understanding.
- The writer encouraged him to trust the Lord completely.
- Trusting in the Lord with his *whole* heart conveys the thought of complete dependence on the Lord in every area of the son's life.
- The son was to acknowledge the Lord in *all* of his ways.
- If the son acknowledged the Lord in all of his ways, his paths would be made straight.
- By using the word "all" as in "all your ways" the writer pointed out that in everything a man does, he should look to God for guidance.
- The word "paths" is plural in verse 6.
- By making the word "paths" plural, the writer conveyed the idea that the son had more than one activity, job or dimension to his life.
- The word "ways" in verse 6 is plural, showing that in all facets of his life the son was to acknowledge God.

Now You Try It!

1. Take John 3:16 for your word study.

2. Select a few of the key words in the verse for special observation.

3. For each word make a list of observations. Consider what the word could possibly mean (semantic range), how John used it in this passage, and what it probably meant here.

4. Using different English translations may help you to make additional observations.

Observation of words helps us to see in detail what the writer was trying to communicate. This is a good start, but we can go even deeper in our search.

Key Points to Remember

🔑 Most words can mean several things in a language. All of these possible meanings taken together equal the word's **semantic range**.

🔑 Observation tries to determine what the writer intended to communicate, and not to read into the text what the reader thinks.

🔑 The **usage** of the word in its immediate context is the best indicator of its intended meaning.

Questions for Reflection

1. Why is it important to understand what a word *could* mean before trying to decide what it *did* mean in a passage?

2. Why is considering the context important in understanding the meaning of words?

3. Why can understanding the words of the Bible be difficult?

4. Why do people often jump to wrong conclusions about the meaning of words in the Bible?

5. How will observing words make you a better Bible student?

Lesson 4

Digging into Words

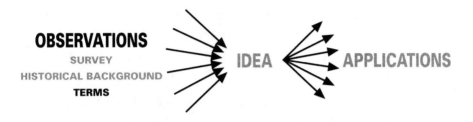

OBSERVATIONS
SURVEY
HISTORICAL BACKGROUND
TERMS
IDEA
APPLICATIONS

Greek to Me

Observing the English text of the Bible is an excellent start in Bible study. Our English translations are usually quite reliable, so when we examine the English terms, we can make many useful and accurate observations. However, any translation is still a translation of the original language, and every translation is somewhat imprecise.

In order to gain the maximum understanding of the Bible, we need to comprehend what the Bible meant in its original languages. You may think, "That's impossible! I could never understand Greek and Hebrew!" Well, you may be surprised how much Greek and Hebrew you can learn when you know what tools to use.

A group of books called **lexical aids** are designed to give the meanings of terms. Using lexical aids takes us from the English translation to the Greek and Hebrew terms of the Bible. Comparing the English with the original terms is like moving from black and white photos to color photos. Now we are able to observe the terms in their original shades of meaning. That view opens a whole new world of understanding for us.

From the King James Version to the Greek Text

Because the King James Version has been used so long, a large number of lexical aids have been developed for it. We can follow these steps to get the meaning of the Greek terms translated in the King James Version:

1. Look up the English term in *Strong's Exhaustive Concordance*. This

concordance has each word in the Bible listed in alphabetical order. It lists each verse that uses the word. A number follows each entry.

2. Look up the number in the Greek dictionary in the back of *Strong's*. The Greek word, an English transliteration of the word and the semantic range of the term in Greek follow the number.

3. Consult other lexical aids to get additional information about the word. The following are especially helpful:

> Colin Brown. *New International Dictionary of New Testament Theology*. Grand Rapids: Zondervan, 1975.

> Larry Richards. *Expository Dictionary of Bible Words*. Grand Rapids: Zondervan, 1985.

> W. E. Vine. *An Expository Dictionary of Biblical Words*. Nashville: Thomas Nelson, 1984.

4. Record your information about the semantic range of the word.

5. Explain how the word is used in this particular passage.

EXAMPLE
"Ordain" in Titus 1:5

1. On page 759 of *Strong's Exhaustive Concordance*, this listing comes under the word "ordain":
Ti 1:5 an*cb*° elders in every city, as I   *2525

2. The Greek dictionary in the back of *Strong's* has this listing:

> *2525.* καθιστημι **kathistemi**, *kath-is'-tay-mee* from *2596* and *2476*; to *place down* (permanently), i.e. (fig.) to *designate, constitute, convoy:* —appoint, be, conduct, make, ordain, set.

3. Data from other lexical aids:

> Brown, vol. 1, pp. 471, 472—to lead or bring in; appoint, especially to an office or position; bring it to pass that

> Vine, p. 450—from *kata*, "down," or "over against," and *histemi*, "to cause to stand, set," is translated "to ordain" in the KJV of Titus 1:5; Heb. 8:3.

4. Semantic range—to set down permanently, to designate, constitute, appoint, make, ordain

5. Usage in Titus 1:5—In this verse, *kathistemi* means to appoint to a position of leadership.

Now You Try It!

Study the word "grace" in Ephesians 2:8.

1. Look up the word in *Strong's Exhaustive Concordance.* Copy the entry:

2. Find the number of the Greek term in the dictionary in the back of *Strong's,* and copy the listing:

3. Search for data from other lexical aids.

4. Summarize the semantic range of the Greek term translated "grace."

5. Determine the usage of the term in Ephesians 2:8.

From the King James Bible to the Hebrew Text

We can follow a similar process for the Old Testament.

1. Look up the term in *Strong's Exhaustive Concordance*, but this time use the Hebrew and Chaldee Dictionary in the back to locate the semantic range.
2. Consult R. Laird Harris, *Theological Wordbook of the Old Testament [TWOT]* (Chicago: Moody, 1981) for a more detailed discussion of the Hebrew term. The second volume of *TWOT* has a chart that matches the number in *Strong's* with the corresponding article in *TWOT*.
3. Consult other lexical aids, including Richards, Vine and William Wilson, *Old Testament Word Studies* (Grand Rapids: Kregel, 1978).
4. Record your information about the semantic range of the word.
5. Explain how the word is used in this particular passage.

EXAMPLE
"Trust" in Proverbs 3:5

1. This listing comes under the word "trust" on page 1079 of *Strong's Exhaustive Concordance*:

   Pr 3:5 *T* in the Lord with all thine heart   *982

2. In the Hebrew and Chaldee Dictionary in the back of *Strong's* is this listing:

   982 בָּטַח **bâṭach,** *baw-takh'*; a prim. root; prop. to hie for refuge [but not so *precipitately* as 2620]; fig. to *trust*, be *confident* or *sure*:—be bold (confident, secure, sure), careless (one, woman), put confidence, (make to) hope, (put, make to) trust.

3. In *TWOT*, vol. 2, p. 1091, *Strong's* 982 corresponds to *TWOT* 233. The discussion in vol. 1, pages 101 and 102 includes this information:

   BATAH expresses that sense of well-being and security that results from having something or someone in whom to place confidence. It stresses the feeling of being safe or secure. The cause for hope is God's unswerving loyalty. It speaks of confident expectation, not just a wishing. Putting confidence in anything other than God is utterly groundless. Trusting in false security is complacency.

4. Data from other lexical aids:

> Vine, p. 218—to be reliant, trust, be unsuspecting

> Wilson, p. 456—to trust, to confide, to place hope and confidence in any one, to be confident, to be secure without fear

5. Semantic range—to trust, to feel confident, to be bold, to feel secure
6. Usage in Proverbs 3:5—In this verse batah means to have a feeling of confident security in the Lord.

Now You Try It!
Study the word "soul" in Psalm 23:3.
1. Look up the word in *Strong's Exhaustive Concordance*. Copy the entry:

2. Find the number of the Hebrew term in the dictionary in the back of *Strong's,* and copy the listing:

3. Search for data from other lexical aids.

4. Summarize the semantic range of the Hebrew term translated "soul."

5. Determine the usage in Psalm 23:3.

Using Other English Translations

Many modern translations of the Bible also have lexical aids that enable us to go directly to the Greek and Hebrew terms. You may want to check out some of the following:

> Edward Goodrick. *The NIV Complete Concordance.* Grand Rapids: Zondervan, 1981.
>
> *Nelson's Complete Concordance of the Revised Standard Version.* 2d ed. Nashville: Thomas Nelson, 1984.
>
> Robert Thomas. *New American Standard Exhaustive Concordance of the Bible.* Nashville: Holman, 1981.

Key Points to Remember

- All **translations** distort the meanings of words in bringing them over into another language.
- We can understand the meanings of Biblical terms in Greek and Hebrew by using **lexical aids.**
- Working from the King James Bible, *Strong's Exhaustive Concordance* helps us to get to the **semantic range** of the Greek and Hebrew terms.
- We need to identify both the **semantic range** (possible meanings) of the term, and its **specific usage** (actual meaning) in the passage.

Questions for Reflection

1. Why is it important to get back to the Greek and Hebrew terms of the Bible?

2. How are lexical aids an important help in Bible study?

3. Why do many people avoid lexical aids in their study? Are their reasons adequate?

4. How are the semantic range and the specific usage of a word related to each other?

5. What benefits does careful word study have for you as a Bible student?

Lesson 5

Seeing the Structure

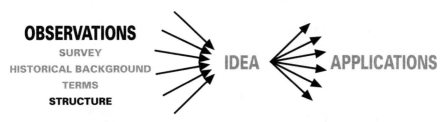

OBSERVATIONS
SURVEY
HISTORICAL BACKGROUND
TERMS
STRUCTURE

IDEA

APPLICATIONS

Seeing How Words Fit Together

When we observe terms, we focus on seeing what each word means by itself. However, the Bible is not just a dictionary, which lists words one at a time. The Bible is a piece of literature, and literature is comprised of meaningful combinations of words. Therefore, our Bible study must not simply generate a list of word studies. We must go beyond observing the individual words to examine how these words are put together.

Visualizing the Literary Structure

For many people, rewriting the passage of Scripture in a form that makes the structure more evident is helpful. This form, called the **mechanical layout,** is only a tool to help us find the elements in the passage. Using a mechanical layout has two benefits. The *process* of constructing the layout forces us to ask how the passage fits together. In addition, the *product* shows at a glance the relationships between the major elements of the passage.

The mechanical layout does not need to be elaborate; in fact, the simpler we keep it, the better. These four steps provide the mechanical layout:

1. Place independent clauses on the left-hand margin. Include the subject, verb and direct object on this line.
2. Place dependent clauses and modifiers under the words they describe.
3. Connect conjunctions by lines to the words and phrases they link.

4. Place your observations and comments about the literary structure in the margins.

EXAMPLE
Philippians 1:9–11

And this I pray
   that your love may abound
             still more and more
             in real knowledge   > and
             in all discernment
       so that you may approve the things
                 that are excellent
             in order to be sincere
                   blameless   > and
             until the day
                     of Christ
        having been filled
          with the fruit
             of righteousness
           which comes
                   through Jesus Christ
                   to the glory   > and
                   praise of God

Now You Try It!

Construct a mechanical layout for Psalm 127. Be sure to follow
the four steps.

Observing the Literary Structure

A writer constructs a piece of literature in the way that will get his message across most effectively. If we can observe *how* the writer puts together his passage, we can understand *what* he is trying to communicate.

Writers use many different techniques in writing. However, several kinds of structure are especially common. If we concentrate on looking for the following kinds of structure, we will see much of what the writer is doing in getting the point across to us.

1. Repetition—Using the *same* term several times in a passage
2. Similarity—Using *similar* words, phrases or ideas
3. Contrast—Using *opposites* to make a point
4. Comparison—Using words such as "like" or "as" to *compare* two items
5. General to Particulars—Moving from a *general* concept (summary or overriding idea) to *particulars* (specific examples of the idea)
6. Particulars to General—Moving from *specific* examples to the *general* idea that summarizes them
7. Cause to Effect—Progressing from a *cause* or *reason* to the *effect* or *result* it produces
8. Effect to Cause—Progressing from an *effect* or *result* to the *cause* or *reason* that produced it
9. Climax—Arranging several items to build to a logical *climax*

41

EXAMPLE
Psalm 1

Repetition

    wicked (vv. 1, 4, 5, 6)

    stand (vv. 1, 5)

    sinners (vv. 1, 5)

    law (v. 2; twice)

    righteous (vv. 5, 6)

    way (v. 6; twice)

Similarity

    wicked, sinners, scoffers (v. 1)

Contrast

    actions of wicked and righteous (vv. 1, 2)

    tree and chaff (vv. 3, 4)

    the Lord's approval and His judgment (v. 6)

Comparison

    righteous like a tree (v 3)

    wicked like chaff (v. 4)

General to Particulars

    how blessed is the man (general) to the particulars that show how he is blessed (vv. 1–3)

    like a tree (general) to the particulars of water, fruit, leaf (v. 3)

Particulars to General

    particulars of water, fruit, leaf to the general truth of prosperity (v. 3)

    verse 6 summarizes the content of the whole psalm

Cause to Effect

    Because he delights in the law (cause), he meditates on it (effect) (v. 2).

    Because the tree is planted by streams of water, it has fruit and leaves (v. 3).

    Because the wicked are like chaff, they will not stand in the judgment (v. 5).

Effect to Cause

Sinners will not stand in the assembly of the righteous (effect), because the Lord knows the way of the righteous (cause) (vv. 5, 6).

Climax

walk to stand to sit (v. 1)
counsel to path to seat (v. 1)
wicked to sinners to scoffers (v. 1)

Now You Try It!

Use your mechanical layout.

Using your mechanical layout of Psalm 127, observe the structural features. See how many examples you can find in each of these categories:

Repetition—

Similarity—

Contrast—

Comparison—

General to Particulars—

Particulars to General—

Cause to Effect—

Effect to Cause—

Climax—

Key Points to Remember

- 🔑 We must treat the Bible as **literature,** not just as a group of words.
- 🔑 Rewriting the passage as a **mechanical layout** can help us visualize how the writer put his words together in meaningful ways.
- 🔑 Writers use many **structural techniques** as they communicate their message. Some of the most frequent types of struc-

ture are repetition, similarity, contrast, comparison, general to particulars, particulars to general, cause to effect, effect to cause, and climax.

Questions for Reflection

1. Why is the observation of structure an important part of Bible study?

2. How can a mechanical layout help us to "see" the passage better?

3. How can structure highlight the point the writer is stressing?

4. How are you growing in your Bible study skills?

5. How does careful Bible study make the Bible come alive to us today?

Summarizing the Subject

What Is the Writer Talking About?

Up to this point, our work in Bible study has focused completely on observing the details of the text. Through the processes of survey reading, superficial reading (learning the historical background), observation of terms and analysis of structure, we can gather large quantities of information. However, all of this data comes as individual pieces. Now we need to put the pieces together into a meaningful whole. We want to discover what the writer is talking about.

The technical term for this step of Bible study is **synthesis**. Another way of referring to this step is determining the writer's **big idea.** This process draws together the observations we have made into a single statement of the writer's main point. Our goal is to summarize the content of the passage in one accurate summary statement.

To discover the big idea, we must know how to look for it. A simple formula can greatly help us:

Subject + Complement = Big Idea

We must define these terms carefully. Often we use the term "subject" to refer to the one who performs an action. However, when we refer to the subject of a passage of Scripture, we are not referring to the *grammatical* subject of a sentence, but rather to what the passage is talking about. This is the *semantic* subject, or the subject of meaning. For example, in the sentence, "The boy hit the ball," the grammatical subject is "boy." After we have identified the semantic subject, we clearly see that the sentence refers not just to the boy, but it also describes the boy's action. Therefore, the semantic subject is *what the boy did.*

We can look at other examples. If we say, "The boy hit the ball over the left field fence," then the semantic subject is *where* the boy hit the ball. "The boy hit the ball during the fourth inning" tells *when* the boy hit the ball. "The boy hit the ball with all his might" describes *how* the boy hit the ball. "The boy hit the ball so that the coach would not kick him off the team" tells *why* the boy hit the ball.

An accurate semantic subject includes three parts. First, it begins with a "pointer" word—who, when, where, what, why or how. The **pointer word** reflects the writer's predominant stress in the passage. The writer had this emphasis in mind when he wrote the verse, paragraph, section or book. If the passage primarily identifies a person or persons, as in Matthew 1:1–16, then the pointer word is *who:* Who the ancestors of Jesus were. When the text concentrates on defining when an action took place, as in Matthew 4:2, the subject begins with *when:* When Jesus was tempted. The *where* pointer word introduces subjects drawn from passages such as Matthew 4:25, in which the location is the central issue: Where the multitude following Jesus came from.

Subjects beginning with "where," "when" or "who" are rare, for few passages have as their primary concern the identification of a person, a time or a location. Most often we will want to use the pointer words "what," "why" and "how." When the text focuses on an action, it uses *what,* as in Matthew 4:23: What Jesus did in Galilee. *Why* begins a subject when the attention centers on the reason or the purpose for an action, as in Matthew 4:1: Why Jesus went into the wilderness. The *how* pointer word indicates that the passage concentrates on the manner or the process by which an action is done. Therefore, Matthew 2:11 describes how: How the wise men greeted the Christ Child.

Second, the pointer word introduces a short statement that summarizes the content of the passage. Ideally, this subject statement should be no longer than ten to twelve words. We want to put the overall content of the passage into a condensed form.

Third, the subject summarizes the content in terms of its original meaning within the literary context. Instead of applying it to today, at this point in our Bible study we need to use "there and then" language. In application, we will get to the here and now, but first we need to understand the passage on its own terms.

EXAMPLES
Matthew 5:16—How the disciples should live before other people

The Greek word *houtos,* translated "so" in the King James Version, is better translated "in such a way" (New American Standard Bible). The verse focuses on *how* the disciples should live in the world. In Matthew 5:1 and 2, Jesus stepped away from the multitude. His disciples went to Him, and He spoke directly to them about how they were to live.

1 Timothy 1:16—Why Paul received God's mercy

Several features in the verse, including "for this reason," show that Paul referred to the reason God had saved him. In this context, Paul gave his personal testimony. Before his salvation, he had rebelled against God and showed hostility toward Christianity. Nevertheless, God saved Paul to use him as an example of how far His mercy to sinners could reach.

Now You Try It!

Determine the subject for John 14:6. Be sure to start the summary statement with the appropriate word, and to put it in "there and then" language.

Synthesizing Larger Units of Scripture

We can develop subject statements for any complete unit of literature. The examples from Matthew 5:16 and 1 Timothy 1:16 show how subjects emerge from single verses. However, we can use the same technique for a paragraph, a section or even an entire book. We simply need to ask, "What is this passage talking about?" As we do this, we must be careful to include *all* of the passage in our subject, rather than focusing on only a part of the passage.

EXAMPLE

Psalm 113

Psalm 113 addresses God's servants. The first part of the psalm (vv. 1–4) exhorts them to praise the Lord continually. The second part (vv. 5–9) gives the reason for that praise. The most comprehensive statement of the message of the entire psalm is "Why God's servants should continually praise the Lord."

Now You Try It!

Looking at Psalm 23 as a whole, state the subject of the psalm. Be sure to start the summary statement with a pointer word and to put the subject in "there and then" language.

Key Points to Remember

- **Synthesis** is the process of drawing together the data discovered in observation into a meaningful whole.
- The **big idea** is a single statement of the writer's main point in a passage.
- The formula for determining the big idea is
  Subject + Complement = Big Idea
- The **subject** summarizes what the passage is talking about. It should have three features:
  1. Start with a **pointer word.**
  rare: who, when, where
  common: what, why, how
  2. Form a short **summary statement** of the content of the passage.
  3. State the subject in **"there and then"** language, that is, in terms of the original audience.
- Remember, we can develop a subject for any complete literary unit: for verses, paragraphs or even for complete books of the Bible.

Questions for Reflection

1. Why is observation by itself inadequate for inductive Bible study?

2. How does the subject help us to appreciate the writer's message?

3. How does synthesis help us to focus our Bible study?

4. Why does the subject stay in "there and then" language?

5. Why is careful observation crucial before we can develop the subject of the passage?

Lesson 7

Expressing the Idea

OBSERVATIONS → IDEA SUBJECT COMPLEMENT ← APPLICATIONS

What Does It Say about the Subject?

The semantic subject summarizes the main point of the passage, but it does not exhaust everything in the text. The passage conveys a message about the subject. This completion of the subject is called the **complement** of the passage.

Once we have defined the subject, it is easy to determine the complement. All we need to do is to take the subject, turn it into a question and then answer it from the passage. That answer is the complement. For example, the subject of Matthew 4:23 is What Jesus did in Galilee. When the subject is transformed into a question, What did Jesus do in Galilee? the complement emerges: *He taught, preached the gospel and healed.* In the same way, the subject of Matthew 4:1 leads to the question, Why did Jesus go into the wilderness? The complement, then, is *to be tempted by the Devil.* The subject of Matthew 2:11 raises the question, How did the wise men greet the Christ Child? The complement, *by worship and gifts,* answers that question.

EXAMPLES
Matthew 5:16
Subject—How the disciples should live before other people
Question—How should the disciples live before other people?
Complement—In such a way that others will glorify God

1 Timothy 1:16
Subject—Why Paul received God's mercy

53

Question—Why did Paul receive God's mercy?
Complement—to be an example of God's long-suffering to sinners

Now You Try It!
John 14:6

Subject—

Question—

Complement—

Psalm 23

Subject—

Question—

Complement—

Putting It All Together

In order to determine the big idea of the passage, we simply need to put the subject and the complement together. This process enables us to state the writer's main point in the passage. The big idea should pass three tests. First, it should be **precise**. In other words, it should accurately summarize the content of the passage. It should not be too narrow, leaving out significant parts of the passage. Neither should it be too broad so that it goes beyond what the passage itself teaches. It should fit the passage as precisely as possible.

Second, it should be **concise**. The big idea is a summary, not a comprehensive discussion of the passage. If we can state the writer's main point in a dozen words or less, we will focus on the heart of the text.

Third, it should attempt to be **memorable**. When we phrase the big idea in a balanced statement, perhaps using rhyme or repeated letters, we can remember it more easily. The statement will stick in our minds longer, and it will help us to communicate the big idea better to others.

Of course, when we refine the big idea to make it concise and memorable, we may have to give up a little precision. This loss is acceptable to a small degree, if it helps us to remember the passage's key point. However, we have to be careful lest our creativity lead us too far from an accurate summary of the text.

EXAMPLES
Matthew 5:16
Subject—How the disciples should live before other people
Complement—in such a way that others will glorify God
Big Idea—The disciples should live before other people in such a way that others will glorify God.
Refined—The disciples' godly practice will bring praise to God.

1 Timothy 1:16
Subject—Why Paul received God's mercy
Complement—to be an example of God's long-suffering to sinners
Big Idea—Paul received God's mercy so that he might be an example of God's long-suffering to sinners.
Refined—Not even Paul was too hopeless for God.

Now You Try It!
John 14:6

Subject—

Complement—

Big Idea—

Refined—

Psalm 23

Subject—

Complement—

Big Idea—

Refined—

The big idea is a key component in Bible study. By defining the subject and complement of the passage and by drawing them together into a precise, concise, memorable statement, we can remain focused on the main point of the text. In addition, we now are ready to make appropriate application of the Bible to life today.

Key Points to Remember

- The **complement** defines what the passage says about the subject.
- We discover the complement by turning the subject of the passage into a **question.** The answer to that question is the complement.
- To state the **big idea**, we put together the subject and the complement. Then we refine it so that the summary statement is **precise, concise** and **memorable**.
- The big idea is important in Bible study because it **pulls together** the observations and **prepares** for applications.

Questions for Reflection

1. Why is it important to determine both the subject and the complement?

2. How can refining the big idea make your Bible study more effective?

3. What would you lose if you did not develop the big idea of the passage?

4. What are the key skills in Bible study that you have learned thus far?

5. Why is it important to understand the writer's big idea in the there and then before moving to applications in the here and now?

Lesson 8

Building a Bridge

OBSERVATIONS → IDEA → **APPLICATIONS**
AUDIENCE ANALYSIS

Are All Applications Created Equal?

How can several people study the same passage of Scripture yet come up with extremely different understandings of how the text should apply to life today? Many times these applications totally contradict each other. How can we say that one application is valid and that another application is invalid?

For example, in the Ten Commandments God commanded His people to keep the Sabbath Day holy (Exod. 20:8–11). The Sabbath Day throughout the Old Testament was Saturday. However, most Christians now treat Sunday in a special way comparable to the Sabbath. Only a small minority insist on keeping Saturday as a day of rest and worship. Does the Old Testament law of Sabbath apply to us today or not, and on what basis do we make that decision?

In the New Testament, we can note Paul's instruction to greet one another with a holy kiss (2 Cor. 13:12). Just think what that greeting could do to liven up a service! Nevertheless, most Christians substitute a cordial greeting or a hearty handshake for the kiss that Paul commanded. Is this substitution what we are to do? How do we decide when to change what is written to make it fit appropriately into our present situation?

After we have completed all the study of observation and have determined the writer's big idea in the passage, we still have to apply the text to life today. The key question of application is this: To what degree is application of this passage to my target audience legitimate? To put it another way, What belongs only to the original context, and what is God's continuing will for the contemporary

59

context? Is this passage relevant to today, or did God intend its message only for the unique situation of its original readers?

Principles for Application

We must follow several important principles to develop valid applications.

First, we must remember that valid application builds on accurate exegesis. Unless we understand what the passage meant there and then to the original audience, we cannot determine what it means in the here and now. If we try to jump immediately into application before looking carefully at the details of the text, we are likely to distort the meaning of the text as we apply it. The original meaning of the text is a standard by which to evaluate applications to different target audiences.

Second, we must recognize the assumptions that we bring to the text. Without realizing it, we all look at the world on the basis of our own situation in life and our background. We read as though we were wearing sunglasses that color everything we see. For this reason sincere students of the Bible can differ widely on the applications they draw. We need to be self-critical so that we realize how we are likely to distort what we find in the Bible. Then we can take special care to compensate for our assumptions as we apply the Scriptures.

Third, we must analyze the distinctive characteristics of the original audience, making use of clues in the historical background and in the context. Most of the Bible was written for specific occasions, not as general theology. For example, in 1 Corinthians chapters 7 and following, Paul responded to a set of questions posed to him by the church in Corinth. In order to understand what Paul meant, we need to comprehend what the Corinthians communicated in their side of the conversation. Paul did not write a comprehensive study of the themes he touched on in those chapters. Instead, he answered the Corinthians' particular questions in a way that would address their unique situation.

In the Old Testament, God gave Israel many laws directing their government, worship and diet. He addressed those commandments to people leaving slavery and wandering in the desert into a new setting of villages, agriculture and political freedom. In addition, the people were surrounded by pagan nations that could tempt them.

Therefore, when we consider how these regulations apply to us today, we must take into consideration the special setting in which God first gave them. Looking carefully at the historical setting of the passage will enable us to understand how it compares or contrasts to our setting today.

Fourth, we must consider clues from other Biblical revelation. Occasionally the Bible itself gives us information that helps us to discern whether the passage is a universal truth or a temporary measure for a specific situation. For instance, Hebrews 9 and 10 have a detailed discussion about how Jesus Christ has superseded the Old Testament sacrificial system. Therefore, Christians today are not under the specific regulations of Leviticus that require animal sacrifices and annual feasts, because Christ's death on the cross brought to an end that whole Old Testament system. What God required of Israel in the past is now obsolete for Christians. In a similar way, in Acts 10:15 the Lord instructed Peter that what the law of Moses had called unclean, God had now made clean. Instead of being under the dietary restrictions of the Old Testament, Christians are now free to eat from the full range of God's creation. God Himself has changed the boundaries of acceptable application.

Fifth, we must bridge the gap between the original audience and the target audience. The **original audience** is the person or group who first received the passage of Scripture. The **target audience** is the person or group to whom the passage is being applied. For example, if we are applying Philippians 2:1–11 to our church, the original audience is the church at Philippi, and the target audience is our church.

When we bridge the gap between the two audiences, we determine the relationship between them. Are the audiences for the most part similar, or do they largely differ from each other? Our application must link the Biblical world with the contemporary world. If we stay in the world of two or three thousand years ago, we cannot have a contemporary application. Neither should we make contemporary applications that are not linked to the original audience. We must bridge the gap between the two worlds.

Determining the Degree of Transfer

The **degree of transfer** is the measure of degree to which the target audience is similar to or different from the original audience.

In order to determine the degree of transfer, we need to evaluate the information we have about the original audience (their identity, their situation, their spiritual level, etc.) and compare the information with what we know about the target audience. For this purpose, it is helpful to construct a chart to plot similarities and differences.

SIMILARITIES	DIFFERENCES

After we have listed the major similarities and differences, we must evaluate them. We must not simply count what we have listed, but rather we must weigh the items to determine how similar or how different the audiences are. It usually helps to plot this evaluation on a number line from 1 to 10.

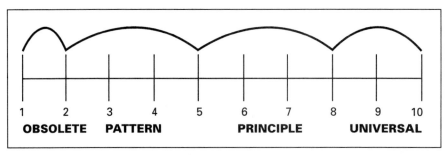

On this number line, 1 and 2 represent passages such as those that explain the Old Testament dietary and sacrificial laws. Those passage address an audience **extremely different from** today's Christians.

A degree of transfer between 2 and 5 may well fit narrative passages that describe what a particular individual did in his unique situation. The character serves as a general **pattern,** but we should not expect to face the exact same challenges.

From 5 to 8 we have the kinds of **principles** found in many of the New Testament epistles. Even though the original readers lived 2,000 years ago and half a world away, they shared many similarities with Christians today.

From 8 to 10 are passages that speak in **universal terms** of God's unchanging attributes or program, or that address a universal human audience of all times.

It is important to remember that a passage of Scripture does not have a single degree of transfer. We can determine the degree of transfer by the relationship between the unchanging original audience of the text and the specific features of the target audience to which the passage is being applied. That statement means that if we apply a passage of the Bible to three target audiences, we will have different sets of similarities and differences for each audience. Therefore, for one target audience the passage could be a principle, for another a pattern and for the third obsolete.

We also need to remember that the assumptions we bring to our application may color how we perceive similarities and differences. Consequently, we always need to be self-critical so that our prejudices do not lead us astray. Listing the similarities and differences helps us to minimize the potential of viewing the Bible through colored lenses.

EXAMPLE
Matthew 5:16

Target Audience—First Christian Church

SIMILARITIES	DIFFERENCES
They are a group of people who desire to follow Christ. They are a diverse group of individuals with a common allegiance to Christ. All godly people thoughout history have been called to point the world to God. The world is watching their lives. Both are related to God as His children.	First Christian Baptist Church is 20th Century; the disciples were 1st century.

Degree of Transfer_____9_____

Now You Try It!

1. Select a passage of Scripture for application.
2. Determine your target audience. You may choose a Christian in-

dividual (such as yourself), a Christian group (your church) or a non-Christian audience.

3. By analyzing the two audiences, determine the similarities and differences between them. List them on a chart.
4. Quantify the degree of transfer on a scale of 1 to 10.

Target Audience _____

SIMILARITIES	DIFFERENCES

Degree of Transfer _____

Key Points to Remember

- **Application** asks how a target audience may appropriately use the passage of Scripture.
- The assumptions we bring to a passage can easily **distort** the applications we find.
- **Audience analysis** looks for similarities and differences between the original audience and the target audience to whom we are applying the passage.
- The **degree of transfer** is a number on a scale of 1 to 10 that measures the degree of similarity between the two audiences.
- A single passage of Scripture may have **different degrees of transfer** for different target audiences.

Questions for Reflection

1. Why do sincere Bible students differ so much in some areas of application?

2. What are some of the presuppositions that you bring to your study of the Bible?

3. Why does accurate observation have to come before valid application?

4. How does audience analysis help to make application more valid?

5. How does this process of application compare with how you have applied the Bible in the past?

Living What We Learn

OBSERVATIONS → IDEA ← **APPLICATIONS**
AUDIENCE ANALYSIS
APPLICATION PRINCIPLE
SMART APPLICATIONS

From Big Idea to Applications

The big idea summarizes what the author communicated to the original audience. It brings together in one sentence what the passage is talking about and what it says about its subject. The big idea is a useful tool for condensing and remembering the main point of the passage.

Although the big idea helps us understand the passage in its original context, it is still stuck in the there and then of the Biblical world. In order to apply the passage to today's audience, we must move from the big idea to applications. We make this move by developing the **application principle**.

The application principle is the big idea restated in terms appropriate for the target audience. By doing audience analysis of the original audience and the target audience, we understand the degree of transfer between the two. Then we can take the big idea, which fits the original audience, and transfer it to the target audience in an appropriate manner.

EXAMPLE
Matthew 5:16

The big idea for Matthew 5:16 is *The disciples' godly practice brings praise to God.* If we want to apply this verse to First Christian Church, we would have a high degree of transfer. Even though the target audience is nearly 2,000 years from the disciples, they are similar in their commitment to Christ and their desire to live for His glory. The degree of transfer from the disciples to First Christian would be around 9. When we restate the big idea in terms of the target audience, the application principle is *First Christian Church's godly practice brings praise to God.*

On the other hand, if we choose a non-Christian target audience, such as the Iraqi army, we would have a low degree of transfer. To state that the Iraqi army's godly practice brings praise to God would be inaccurate. In this case, we would need to adjust the application principle to say that if the Iraqi army were to become committed to Christ, then their godly practice would bring praise to God. The degree of transfer makes all the difference in stating the application principle.

Now You Try It!

Take 1 Timothy 1:16, which has the big idea *Not even Paul was too hopeless for God.* Apply it to two different target audiences, one with a high degree of transfer and the other with a low degree of transfer. State the application principles for each target audience in terms appropriate for the degree of transfer.

First Target Audience _____

SIMILARITIES	DIFFERENCES

Degree of Transfer_____

Second Target Audience _____

SIMILARITIES	DIFFERENCES

Degree of Transfer_____

State the Applications

We come at last to the ultimate purpose of Bible study. We do not study a passage of Scripture to fill our minds with facts or to satisfy our curiosity. God did not give us His Word just to inform us, and certainly not to entertain us. God gave us His Word in order to change our lives. Bible study without application misses the whole point. It is like preparing a meal and never eating a bite.

Good applications do not just happen. We have to work at our applications just as we have worked to get accurate observations, the big idea and the degree of transfer. When we state the applications of the passage for the target audience, we need to keep in mind the following four truths.

First, we must pray for the Holy Spirit's **illumination**. The Bible is God's Word, and God has given us the Holy Spirit to teach us what it means. We Christians have the great advantage of the Holy Spirit's living within us to instruct us constantly concerning the Bible's meaning and its application today.

Second, we need to meditate on the passage. **Meditation** is holding an internal conversation that leads to grasping and living the truth. Psalm 1:2 states that the godly person meditates on God's Word continually. Application involves intense thinking about how, in specific terms, a principle fits into the target audience's experience.

Third, when we write out applications for each target audience, we should make them **SMART** applications: **S**pecific, **M**easurable, **A**ttainable, **R**ealistic and **T**ime-determined. General applications lead only to general obedience. Specific, pointed applications encourage us to obey the passage in practical, life-changing ways.

Fourth, we must determine to **obey the applications**. The best applications are worthless if they stay on paper and never come out in life. We need to remember, "Truth that is learned but not lived forms calluses on the soul." If we get into the habit of knowing what God wants us to do but refusing to do it, we become increasingly insensitive to God's convicting ministry in our lives. That is a real danger in Bible study—knowledge that falls short of action.

EXAMPLE
Matthew 5:16

Big Idea—The disciples' godly practice brings praise to God.

Target Audience—I (a Christian)
Application Principle—My godly practice brings praise to God.
SMART Applications
- I need to take time to greet my neighbor this afternoon.
- I need to call one friend this evening to encourage him during this hard time.
- By the end of the week I need to have at least one significant conversation with an unsaved person.
- I need to keep my lawn in a condition that will please my neighbors and open the door for testimony to them.
- I must keep my speech glorifying to the Lord as I talk with my family and acquaintances.

Now You Try It!
Find the SMART applications for Proverbs 3:5 and 6.
Develop the big idea and then apply it to your life with a list of SMART applications.

Big Idea—

Target Audience—you

Degree of Transfer

Application Principle

SMART Applications

Key Points to Remember

- The **application principle** restates the big idea in terms of the target audience.
- The **goal** of Bible study is **changed lives,** not just increased knowledge.
- To get an accurate application, our minds must **meditate** on the passage as the Holy Spirit **illumines** them.
- To be most effective, applications should be **SMART** (specific, measurable, attainable, realistic and time-determined).
- "Truth that is learned but not lived forms calluses on the soul."

Questions for Reflection

1. How does the application principle link together observation and application?

2. Why is the teaching ministry of the Holy Spirit vital to application?

3. How does meditation aid in the process of application?

4. Why is it important to make applications SMART?

5. How can learning the Bible harden us in our spiritual lives?

Staying in the Word

OBSERVATIONS   **IDEA**   **APPLICATIONS**

SURVEY   SUBJECT+   AUDIENCE ANALYSIS

HISTORICAL BACKGROUND   COMPLEMENT=   APPLICATION PRINCIPLE

TERMS   BIG IDEA   SMART APPLICATIONS

STRUCTURE

Putting It All Together

In the first chapter of this manual, we noted that the ideal procedure of Bible study has four components: maximum accuracy, maximum application, joy of personal discovery and reasonable time. In learning the skills of inductive Bible study you have become equipped to understand what a passage meant in its original context and what it means for a variety of target audiences today. By doing the study yourself, you have had the joy of discovering what God has to teach in His Word. However, you probably have wondered how you can use this method in a reasonable amount of time.

Once you have learned a skill well, you can use the essential aspects of that skill in a relatively small amount of time. Even if you are unable to use every technique that you could if you had unlimited time available, you can still do excellent work. We can compare Bible study to a pyramid (see figure).

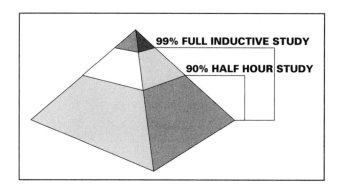

99% FULL INDUCTIVE STUDY

90% HALF HOUR STUDY

If you are skillful in the techniques of inductive Bible study, in the first half hour you can probably understand up to 90 percent of the key content of the passage. When you use the full range of your skills in observing the passage, synthesizing it into the big idea and applying it to a specific target audience, you may well move from 90 percent to 99 percent understanding. The remaining one percent is the portion about which scholars argue. Some words are nearly impossible to define precisely with our present state of knowledge. Some points of grammar will remain ambiguous. There will be interpretive questions that no one can fully answer this side of Heaven.

Of course, we should aspire to learn as much as we can of God's Word. However, we must also use our time and minds in the most efficient way. That means we should focus our attention on the **90 percent half-hour** study. We can follow this pattern the rest of our lives. By spending 30 minutes daily on inductive study, we can learn a large portion of the truth God wants us to know. Then, when we have opportunity to dig deeper, we can use the entire inductive process we have learned to scrutinize the Scriptures.

To make the most effective use of 30 minutes in studying a passage of Scripture, we need to organize our work. It would be helpful to take about 15 minutes to observe the passage, quickly noting the historical background and then focusing on understanding the key terms and major structural features. At that point, we might briefly use a lexical aid or a commentary to help us. Then we could take about five minutes to determine the subject and complement and put them together into a precise, concise, memorable big idea. We could take the remaining ten minutes to apply the passage to our own lives or to the target audience we have in mind.

Now You Try It!
Using just 30 minutes, do an inductive study of Hebrews 4:14–16.
1. Observations (15 minutes)

2. Synthesis (5 minutes)

3. Applications (10 minutes)

Passing It On to Others

Now that you have learned how to study the Bible on your own, you need to share this skill with others. You will find that when you teach someone else how to observe, synthesize and apply God's Word, you will share the blessing that you have received. What we learn, we must live and then pass on to others.

Key Points to Remember

- Once you have developed **skill** in inductive Bible study, you can focus on efficiency and can pick up **speed**.
- In **30 minutes** a skilled Bible student can learn up to **90 percent** of the content of a passage.
- Using the full inductive process will enable you to learn up to **99 percent** of a passage of Scripture.
- Some features of the Bible may always lie beyond our understanding. They are important for scholars to investigate, but it is better for most Bible students to focus on using our time most **efficiently.**
- Productive Bible study needs to maintain a balance among **observation, synthesis** and **application.**

Questions for Reflection

1. Why is the 90 percent half-hour procedure appropriate for most Christians?

2. In what situations will you probably want to use the full inductive process?

3. How does the pyramid model link together the unique contributions of pastors and teachers, scholars, and laymen and laywomen?

4. How has the inductive method of Bible study affected how you investigate God's Word?

5. How do you plan to use the inductive method in your own study in the future?

Glossary

Analytical approach: The method of study that focuses on observing the details of the text. It may not grasp the big picture or apply the passage to life today.

Application principle: The big idea restated in terms of the target audience

Big idea: A precise, concise and memorable statement of the key concept in the passage

Clause: A group of words containing a subject and a verb or verbal form. A clause is longer than a phrase and usually shorter than a complete sentence

Climax: A series of words or actions that build to a point of emphasis.

Commentaries: Books that interpret and discuss a piece of literature

Comparison: An illustration of a concept by using a word picture, such as "The Lord is my *shepherd.*"

Complement: What the passage says about the subject. To find the complement, turn the subject into a question; the answer is the complement.

Conjunctions: Words such as *and* or *but,* which connect words or phrases

Contrast: Words or phrases that form a set of opposites

Dependent clause: A clause that cannot stand alone. It needs to depend on an independent clause.

Devotional approach: The method of study that focuses on personal application. It may read into the text what the reader thinks rather than discussing what the text really means.

Eisegesis: Reading the reader's ideas into the text

Exegesis: Leading the author's meaning out of the text

Independent clause: A clause that can stand on its own. It usually has a subject, a verb and an object.

Inductive Bible study: The process of Bible study that observes the passage, draws the observations into the big idea and then applies the idea to life today

Lexical aids: Books that help in understanding the precise meanings of words

Literary context: The passage immediately surrounding a text of literature

Literary structure: The way that a piece of literature is put together using the laws of composition

Mechanical layout: A rewriting of a passage to highlight its literary structure

Meditation: Reflecting on a concept until it is applied to life

Modifiers

> **adjectives:** Words that describe a person, place or thing
>
> **adverbs:** Words that describe how an action takes place
>
> **prepositional phrases:** Phrases beginning with words such as *in, for,* and *during* that describe things or actions

Morpheme: A basic building block of meaning

90 percent half-hour study: Using the basic technique of inductive Bible study to grasp the general context and application of a passage in a short period of time. It consists of 15 minutes of observations, 5 minutes of synthesis and 10 minutes of applications.

Original audience: The people for whom the passage was first written or spoken

Phoneme: A basic building block of sound

Pointer word: The word that begins the subject and determines the focus of the passage. Rare pointer words are who, when and where. Common pointer words are what, why, how.

Semantic: Refers to meaning

Semantic range: The total quantity of what a word could mean in a language

SMART: Applications that are Specific, Measurable, Attainable, Realistic and Time-determined

Subject statement: A short summary of what the passage is talking about. It starts with a pointer word and is put in "there and then" language.

Synthesis: Pulling the observations together into the big idea

Target audience: The person or persons to whom a passage of the Bible is being applied

Translation: Putting the Hebrew and Greek words of the original Biblical text into another language.

Transliteration: Replacing a word in the letters of another language. For example, the Greek word καθιστημι is rewritten as *kathistemi*.

Universal audience: A group that includes all people at all times

To remind you of the Bible-study process, you may want to cut out the diagram below, paste it onto a card and keep it in your Bible.

OBSERVATIONS   IDEA   APPLICATIONS
SURVEY   SUBJECT+   AUDIENCE ANALYSIS
HISTORICAL BACKGROUND COMPLEMENT=   APPLICATION PRINCIPLE
TERMS   BIG IDEA   SMART APPLICATIONS
STRUCTURE